AN ANTHOLOGY OF DALIT LITERATURE
(POEMS)

An Anthology of DALIT LITERATURE

(Poems)

Editors

Mulk Raj Anand

Eleanor Zelliot

GYAN

Published by

Gyan Publishing House
5, Ansari Road
Daryaganj, New Delhi-110002
Phone: 011-47034999, 9811692060
E-mail: books@gyanbooks.com

Distribution Network
gyanbooks.com
India, USA, Canada, UK, Australia, France

ISBN: 978-81-212-0419-4 (HB)

Reprint in India, 2024
First Published, 1992

Printed at: Gyan Press, Delhi.

An Anthology of Dalit Literature
Editor: Mulk Raj Anand, Eleanor Zelliot

CONTENTS

Some Words by way of Preface to Dalit Poems

Mulk Raj Anand

Poetry is passion !

Its origins lie in rhythmic expression of cries by our early ancestors, as they thumped on earth and danced before going out to kill the beast for food. The shouts were magic by which the dancers wished to impose their will onto the beast and get/a goodkill !

Later, the folk mimed the process of sowing and reaping the mime of rain and the wind, and the blossoming of crops.

Dance and song inspired the tiller to work with greater energy on furrowing the land, the weeding, the watering and the reaping !

Rhythmic speech, then, which is poetry has grown out of extroversion of physical energy to achieve desired reality.

Incantation achieves rhythm from the heightened flow of blood in the body which compels the soul to utter prophecy.

Alliterative effect comes from repetition of

metaphor made by fantasy relating innner wish to outer phenomena in verbal expression.

An old Irish mantic utterance may illustrate magic become poem :

"Good tidings : sea fruitful, wave -
washed stand, smiling woods !
Witchcraft flees, orchards blossom,
Cornfields ripen, bees swarn
A cheerful world, peace and plenty, happy summer!"

It is from the core of the heart that feeling arises : heart beat may become rhythm of one - two, urging vibrations of the vocal chords in the grunt, the grumble, or the gush !

The cry beomes invocation often when men and women labour

'Hia ! Hia !' is repeated together in charm by the pullers of the cart of the diayllabic labour cry--

An African boy was heard by a Christian Missionery to be singing words while breaking stones by the dusty track to make a road:

' They treat us badly ehe' !
They are hard on us ehe !

They drink their coffee ehe !
And give us none, ehe !'

Ofcourse, the poems into which thought processes enter evolve in the subtle artifice of prosody. But even in sophisticated rhythms one can sometimes see the movement of the hand, in the expression of feeling, in singing words of our primitive forefather, the tribal bard.

The process of poetry arising out of the cry can be felt in most Dalit poems, because in these utterances protest seems to come from the insulted and the injured, who have laboured for generation for the supers, thier hands with dirty work. One can take almost any Dalit poem and feel the cry rhythm arising from itself

I quote the poem Revolution by Arjun Dangle :

"We used to be their friends
When clay pots hung from our necks
Brooms tied to our rumps
We made our rounds through the Upper Lane
Calling 'Johar Maybap"!

OR

Notice the cry of Namdev Dhassal in his poem, *'So that my mother may be convinced :'*

A body broken down for seven generations
Gentle mother, your feet haven't travelled
through the ten continents,
you never, never, never could leave your
village world".......

Again :

' Mother, remember your troubled life,
The start of your life --
That day you were new bride, anointed with tumeric
had come ceremoniously to your father-in law's
house
How many wishes, how many hopes, were in
your mind
From then to now -- dragged through life
Mother-doesn't it gnaw you ?'

OR

the poem *Eklavya* !

O ! Eklavya !
The round earth
        You ideal disciple !
A steel lever in my hand
        Give me the finger you cut off
But no leverage?

That will be my fulcrum !'

In the poems where thought enters, we notice that both content and form have internal coherance of their own, and become prose-poem.

I quote from Daya Pawar's *Buddha* :

"I never see you in Jeta's garden
Sitting with eyes closed
In meditation, in the lotus position

OR

"In the caves of Ajanta and Ellora
with stone tips sewn shut
sleeping the last sleep of your life I see you
walking, talking, breathing, softly breathing
on the sorrows of the poor, the weak !
Going from hut to hut
In the life destroying darkness !
Torch in hand giving to sorrow !
That drains the blood like a continuous disease-
a new meaning"

Dalit poetry, then, seems to derive its power from labour protest : Personal words entry the prosodic processes of so-called 'Classical' poetry which is itself emergent from folksong and heroic epic, as in Mahabharat or in Homer's Odyssey, above contemporary rhythmic conversational speech.

On surface, it seems rhythms have become strain, as in elaborate symphonies of Beethovan, or in our own Pukka Raags, by the cry or urge going deep into the body soul. And by repetition of strains, the inner urge stir diarythmls in continuous rhythms, varied and evocative of a mood, either of the *Adbhuts* Rasa or *Sringara* or one of the nine Navarasas of Bharata.

Unknown to the poets of the middle sections of society, who have emerged from literate traditions of Sanskrit language or from the European, particularly English lyric, of Shelley or the epic of Milton, *Paradise Lost,* the Dalits poets between the poem as magic cry, or fantasy of fulfilment of the wish to change the human condition of contempt for men and women, by the self-appointed upper Brahmins and their followers in the Varnashram caste order.

The attitude of these poets is revolutionary!

The outcastes are crying against deaf gods, questioning God Brahma Himself. And their despair asserts itself in ringing triumphs of throwing off the yoke.

Quite unconsciously in the passion of these

posts for the desired change in the human relations, there is. a Shakespearan ring. I re-call the sonnet of the Elizabethan bard :

"When in disgrace with fortune and men's eyes
I all alone beweep my outcast state,
And trouble deaf human with my bootless cries
and look upon myself, and curse my fate,
Wishing me like, to one more rich in hope.
Featured like him, like him with friends possest,
Desiring this man's art, and that man's scope
With what I most enjoy contented least
Yet in these thoughts myself almost despising
I think on thee, and then my state.
Like to the lark at break of lay arising
From sullen earth, sings hymns at heavens gate
For thy sweet love remembered such wealth brings
That then I scron to change my state with kings.

I do not wish to put the Dalit poets to invicious comparisons.

But they are emergent, in our time of renewal, from the old dacayed society, from the dead-past surviving as Brahmanical ritual or Islamic taboo and blind faith in the big bearded God sitting on top of the sky, into the light is Buddha's eyes. And they have the force and vivacity of deep agonies against the rejection of themeselves, and a hundred million Untouchables, in their pulsing hearts, behind the words !

Let them be judged from the impact of their anguish, their aspiration to breathe freely the air, without praying to be allowed to crawl on earth on which they are born by calling out 'Posh ! Posh !' untouchable coming ! Let them lift their heads- up to the Sun, the moon and the stars, looking for light!

MULK RAJ ANAND

Khandalla
Dist Pune
Mahrashtra

DALIT SAHITYA
The Historical Background

Eleanor Zelliot

The Dalit Sahitya (literature of the oppressed) movement in Maharashtra seems to be unique - not in the phenomenon of former Untouchables writing literature, but in the quantity of writing, its variety, its aesthetic considerations, its sense of being a movement, its tie to social action, and in the serious attention it receives as a school within the Marathi literary traditions: Parallel movements in Dalit writing have now appeared in the neighbouring states of Karnataka and Gujarat, and Dalit Sahitya may someday be an all-India movement.

The meaning of *dalit* in Hindi and Marathi is "ground down, depressed", and is now used by politicised Untouchables in preference to any other designation. The term is one of pride - Untouchables have been oppressed by others; there is nothing inherently wrong with them. Their insistence on the use of Dalit has been recognised officially, and the state governments of Maharashtra, Madhya Pradesh and Uttar Pradesh have issued orders that *Dalit* be the term used, rather than Harijan, Scheduled Caste, or Untouchable.

Dalit creativity in all its phases is closely tied to the movement begun by the Mahar caste before the turn of this century. Dr. B.R. Ambedkar came to dominate this movement in the 1920's, and its current achievements and stance, as well as the predominantly Buddhist belief of the movement's members, are due to his shaping. To discuss Dalit Sahitya as a historical phenomenon, then, means we must look at the Mahar movement, the Buddhist conversion and the aims of Dr. Ambedkar.

The Mahars, a large Marathi speaking caste now eighty per cent Buddhist and disclaiming caste, had a traditional role of "inferior village servant," as the British called them. They constituted about nine per cent of the population of the Marathi speaking area in western India, and were found in every village throughout Maharashtra. Their traditional work was to serve the village as watchmen, removers of dead cattle, messengers, i.e. all-purpose servants but with some very responsible duties. They also were traditionally the singers, dancers, comedians and drummers of the folk drama eg. *Tamasha*. Along with the other untouchable castes in the area, Mangs and Chambhars, the well and temple were closed to them, and their living quarters were removed from the village proper. Before the 19th century the only recorded voice of the Mahar was that of Chokhamela, a 14th century poet-saint within the devotional religious tradition called Bhakti. Although beloved by other poet-saints, Chokhamela lived as a traditional village Mahar.

Although many of Chokhamela's poems sing of the glory of the God Vitthal and meaning of devotion, some do protest against untouchability. Others acknowledge social inferiority and find comfort in religious equality, such as this *abhanga*, which is very popular today:

> The sugarcane may be crooked but its juice is not!
> Why are you deceived by the way things look?
>
> The bow may be curved but the arrow is straight.
> Why are you deceived by the way things look?
> The river may be winding but its water is not crooked.
>
> Why are you deceived by the way things look?
>
> Chokha may be ill-shaped, but not his God Vitthal.

Why are you deceived by the way things look?

There is, however, one poignant cry against the very idea of pollution, of untouchability:

The only impurity is in the five elements.
There is only one substance in the world.
Then who is pure and who is impure?
The cause of pollution is in the creation of the body.
In the beginning,
At the end,
There is nothing but pollution.
No one knows anyone who is born pure.
Choka asks , in wonder
Who is pure?

Between Chokhamela and the beginning of the modern movement, there is no literature other than remembered legends and myths. The first document of the new movement, however, is not only a full blown indictment of the caste hierarchy sanctioned by scripture, but also bears with it a poem of protest. The dominant figure in this early period was Gopal Baba Walangkar, an ex-soldier and a Mahar, who started a newspaper, publicly challenged caste Hindu about their treatment of Untouchables, and petitioned the British

Government to allow the recruitment of Untouchables into the army, a practice which had been stopped about 1890. A copy of the handwritten petition, dated 1894, lies in the Khairmode collection of Ambedkar materials in the Bombay University Library. Attached to the document is a poem, a remarkable combination of plain bitter Marathi and Sanskritized

Marathi terms, of descriptions of the degradation forced upon the Mahars by Hindu practice, even criticism of those Mahars who exploit their brethren. Who the author, one "Pandit Kondiram," was is not known, but his is the first poetic *Dalit* voice, and it is as full of protest as that of any modern *Dalit* poet. He concludes a haunting description of the conditions of Untouchables with :

> Keep the memory of our age-long suffering in your minds.
> When you see a human animal, have a little pride!
> Burn the Brahman scriptures and give a true message!
> This is the warning of Pandit Kondiram.

Within ten years of Walangkar's petition, a whole generation of leadership had sprung up, urging those

Mahars who had left the village for work in the mills, on the railroads, on the docks, to educate themselves and to organize to gain strength. While Walangkar and other early leaders were from the Bombay and Pune areas, Nagpur also formed a strong part of the movement. Kisan Fago Bansode left a small volume of poetry along with his work for newspapers, libraries, conferences, petitions and educational institutions in that area. One poem is very critical, in spite of Bansode's own devout Hinduism:

Look, look, all people. This is my Hindu nation.
Divided at its root,
a jungle of divisions.

Honour for enmity - this is my Hindu nation.
Nowhere in the world
such segregation as here.

Caste at birth. This is my Hindu nation.
High place to the Brahman,
low to all others.

The seed of this is in religion. This is my Hindu nation.

In another poem, Bansode invokes the figure of the saint-poet Chokhamela to inspire a new spirit:

Why do you endure curses?
Chokha went into the temple resolutely.
Why do you, ashamed, stay away?
You are the descendants of Chokha.
Why do you fear to enter the temple?
Come, take a stance like a wrestler,
Together let us conquer pollution.

Twenty years after Bansode and the equally important leader from Pune, Shivram Janba Kamble, began their work, a leader arose who was much better educated, even more capable in spreading a modern message of equality, one who could spread the movement far beyond the Mahar caste. Dr. B.R. Ambedkar (1891-1956) was a distant relative of Walangkar and took pride in the army background of Walangkar and his own father. Brought to Bombay by his ambitious father, and aided by reform-minded Maratha princes who saw in his bright Untouchable student a chance to enhance the anti-Brahman movement, Ambedkar secured a B.A. from Elphinstone College in Bombay, a Ph.D. from Columbia University in New York, a D.Sc. from London and the designation of Barrister from Grey's Inn. He was not only by far the most highly educated Untouchable in India, he probably held more degrees than any Brahman in the Maharashtra area. He represented all that the Untouchable could hope to be, he remained identified with his people, and he was extraordinarily competent in securing rights from the British Government as it began to democratize its parliamentary structures in India.

Ambedkar's own vast amount of writing is primarily political, but the organizations and the spirit which he created are at the root of the new literary movement. From 1920 on he published newspapers, at times including poetry or a story. But chiefly the newspapers were a channel for communication, their contents spreading somehow among a people whose literary rate was less than three per cent. The newspapers themselves were symbols of achievement, and while Ambedkar's dominated, there were many others. It is significant that in 1962 A.S. Ranpise published a list of every newspapers started by an Untouchable in India, beginning with Walangkar's short lived effort and finally totally one hundred twenty, the great majority of them in Marathi.

Even more important in terms of literature, Ambedkar's leadership not only stressed the importance of education but also provided opportunities for both students and teachers. The final result of years of work, beginning with hostels and pleas for scholarship aid, is a vast system of financial help for the "Scheduled Castes" from the government and also a system of educational institutions run by members of the movement themselves. Ambedkar's People's Education Society and other similar groups in Maharashtra maintain over a dozen college complexes, and one Ambedkar follower has created a medical college in Karnataka. These colleges not only educate but also provide literary circles and to some degree employment for the highly educated ex-Untouchable. (Ex-because the Constitution of India prohibits the practice of untouchability.) It is not an accident that the chief organ of Dalit literature, *Asmitadarsh* (mirror of identity), was founded in 1968 by Gangadhar Pantawane, then a professor of Marathi at Ambedkar's Milind College of Arts in Aurangabad.

Ambedkar's political work, which was the base of the movement, must be given short shrift here as a subject too complex for easy generalization. Two notes will have to suffice. First, Ambedkar's followers down to the village level are highly politicized. Second, Ambedkar's political parties, always opposed to the Indian National Congress, found no way to attract enough non-Untouchable voters to develop a useful power base. Most writers today are outside organized politics. The vital concern with politics, however, may be seen in the development of the Dalit Panthers, an organization founded in 1972 by writers to protest both atrocities against Untouchables in the villages and the ineffectiveness of the Republican Party, founded by Ambedkar just before his death in 1956. The Dalit Panthers, named after the Black Panthers in the United States, is still in existence, although its effective militant stance has been reduced by splits in leadership and by its inability to curb village violence. The founders of the Panthers, Namdeo Dhasal and Raja Dhale, were poets, committed both to literature and to literature as a weapon against social justice. The headline years of the Panthers, 1972-73, may also be said to mark the true beginning of the Dalit Sahitya movement, although individual writers had appeared earlier.

Another area of Ambedkar's leadership, that of religious conversion, may be just as important a factor in the development of Dalit Sahitya as education and politics. While the newspapers may be seen as a symbol of organized communication, the educational institutions as opportunity, and the political stress as an urge to participate in government, the conversion to Buddhism provided psychological freedom. The Buddhist conversion of 1956 marked not only the rejection of untouchability but also the whole system of gods, myths, rebirth, pollution and caste, which were seen as the base of that practice. Buddhism was seen as rational and humanitarian and also as a religion which stressed the mind and creativity.

The Buddhist conversion came almost thirty years after a great "satyagraha" for water at Mahad in 1928, an event which many use as a poetic image for protest, and after years of fruitless attempts at temple entry. It came after it became clear that independent India's new Constitution, which Dr. Ambedkar helped frame as Chair of the Drafting Committee, could outlaw untouchability but not remove the idea of pollution and hierarchy from hearts and minds. Chokhamela's protest from within the system, Bansode's critical love for Hinduism, were rejected as no longer adequate for men and women who wanted social and psychological freedom .Gangadhar Pantawane, the Dalit journal editor, once wrote to me in a letter, "To me, Dalit is not a caste. He is a man exploited by the social and economic traditions of this country. He does not believe in God, Rebirth, Soul, Holy Books teaching separatism, fate and Heaven because they have made him a slave. He does believe in humanism. Dalit is a symbol of change and revolution." Baburao Bagul, a major short story writer, dates the beginning of Dalit Sahitya from the Buddhist conversion of 1956.

Before the Buddhist conversion, there was "movement literature"- polemics, biography, folk songs and poems in abundance, all intended to further the cause of equality. The "street" literature still continues, slim booklets sold at conferences and on Buddha Jayanti and Ambedkar Jayanti, its subjects generally the life and work of Ambedkar and of the Buddha. Indeed folk poetry has reached a new height in the songs of Waman Kardak, who moves among the Buddhist community singing songs of Ambedkar and the Buddha, of the events which are milestones in the movement. The literary work which is Dalit Sahitya at first rarely dealt with Buddhism or praised Ambedkar. Its aim was to distil experience into words, to use language to capture experience and suffering never before recorded. It rarely uses the caste name Mahar, even though most of the poets, novelists and short story writers are former Mahars. It records the history of the movement only when an event, such as the burning of the Brahmanical law book, the Manusmriti, at Mahad in 1928, stands as an image for an idea. More recently, Buddhist references are to be found increasingly in the poetry as that identity is more and more thoroughly internalizes. And in the light of Ambedkar's continuing and ever increasing importance, there is now almost enough poetry about "Babasaheb" Ambedkar to warrant a book on that subject alone.

Within two years of the conversion, the first major figure in Dalit Sahitya, Shankarrao Kharat, published a book of short stories; *Bara Balutedar* appeared in 1958. In it each of the servants of the traditional village, including the Mahar "inferior village servant," to use that telling British phrase, is the subject of a gentle character sketch. Kharat now has two dozen or so books to his credit, including an edition of Ambedkar's letters and a history of the Buddhist conversion. But his main thrust is the description of the life of the Mahar and of other lowly people in the traditional village. His writing is sad but not bitter, descriptive rather than analytical. A different style appeared soon after Kharat with Baburao Bagul, whose short stories are much more forceful, often based on city life, more realistic in their descriptions of violence and vulgarity. A third early figure reflects another facet of Dalit literature. Annabhau Sathe's stories and novels contain images of the untouchable Mang as here, as leader in the battles against the British. Sathe's political position was closer to the Communist Party than to Ambedkar's parties, although one of his major books is dedicated to Ambedkar. As a Mang, Sathe suffered the same deprivations as other Untouchables, but like most Mangs, he did not participate in Ambedkar's movement, nor the Buddhist conversion. Although Sathe was and is highly respected, his type of heroic literature seems to be an isolated phenomenon.

In the late 1960's, the trickle of Dalit writing

became a flood. The highly regarded Marathi journal *Marathwada* featured Dalit writing in a 1969 issue. By November 25, 1973, the Bombay *Times of India* could give over a special *Times Weekly* issue entirely to Dalit poetry and stories, translated into English. In his introduction to the issue, Dileep Padgakar wrote":

"Despite [its] limitations, Dalit literature remains an authentic breakthrough in the otherwise dreary literary scene in the country. Its immense merit is to have effectively rebelled in life as in letters, against the middle-class Hindu who have monopolized cultural expression":

The revolt of which Padgaonkar wrote was that of the Dalit Panthers, and it is with them that Dalit poetry becomes one of the most important strands in recent Marathi literature. Five of the founding members of the Panthers are represented in this collection. Namdeo Dhasal (1949-) was Defence Minister, J.V. Pawar (1944) was General Secretary, Arun Kamble (1952) and Arjun Dangle (1945-) were ardent young members of that first group, Prahlad Chendvankar (1937) slightly older. (The Panther President, Raja Dhale, has continued in art and design rather than poetry.) Although the original Panthers split in 1974, all are still active in some form of creativity. The most prominent poet in Dalit

Sahitya is Namdeo Dhasal, whose language is both the most shocking and the most innovative of all.

Other poets emerged outside the Panther group, and while the opposition to Hindu traditional treatment of Untouchables was just as strong, the tone and speech of the three slightly older poets represented here is gentler, more optimistic. Daya Pawar (1935-) not only published poetry but wrote a somewhat fictionalized autobiography which he titled *Balut*, the name of the arrangement by which the Mahar in the village performed his traditional work. *Balut* was widely praised and was very influential, and the writing of autobiographies is now an important feature of Marathi literature, not only among Buddhists but also in other Dalit groups. Tryambak Sapkale (1930) published *Surung* (explosion) in 1976, and immediately won the poetry prize in Marathi for the year. Waman Nimbalkar (1939-), published his first, romantic, poem in 1959, but by 1973, he titled his *dalit* poetry collection *Gaokushabaheril kavita* (poetry from the outskirts of the village).

Two of the poets here are in academic professions. Keshav Meshram (1937-) is a professor of Marathi literature in Bombay and has edited the most important collection of Dalit poetry: *Vidrohi kavita* (poetry in opposition), published by Continental Prakashan in Pune in 1978, with an expanded edition in 1987. Yeshwant Manohar 1951, whose Ph.D. in Marathi literature is from Nagpur University, is now head of the premier Marathi literature council in Bombay. One poet in the volume is neither Buddhist, nor Panther, nor academic : Narayan Surve (1926-) was an orphan in Bombay, casteless as well as homeless. A staunch Communist, he writes as easily about Karl Marx as about Hindu religious concepts. His poetry is important enough to warrant a volume of his collected works, published by Lokwangmaya Graha in 1982.

The most recent trend in the ever-changing field of Dalit literature is the increasing importance of women poets. Hira Bansode (1939-) has an M.A. in Marathi, is a clerk in the railway in Bombay, and has become a feminist as well as a staunch Ambedkarite. Mina Gajbhiye (1957-), I am told, died after composing a number of very moving poems. Dr. Jyoti Langewar (1950) teaches in Nagpur. I found the poems by Anuradha Gaurav and Mina Londe in *Asmitadarsh*, the Dalit literary journal published in Aurangabad, but know nothing about the poets. Women have also entered the autobiographical field, and two Buddhist women with marginal educations have published their autobiographies in Marathi.

There are many more creative poets in the Dalit school. Keshav Meshram includes 37 in his collection of Dalit poetry. To those poets whose work would add to this collection but whom I have not been able to include, I offer my apologies.

Although I am not in the field of literature, I have gathered together this collection because of my interest in all the facets of the Ambedkar movement, and I have found the poetry an excellent reflection of the values and accomplishments of that movement. As a historian, I know the context of the poetry, but I am neither particularly accomplished in Marathi nor a poet, and I have relied heavily on Jayant Karve. We have sat together many hours, arguing, laughing, sorrowing, wondering over these poems, with some occasional felicitous suggestions from two friends who know no Marathi but who are published poets: A.K. Ramanujan and Pam Espeland. For the earlier translations of *Chokhamela* and Kisan Fago Bansode, I have had important help from Maxine Berntsen, B.S. Shinde and Rekha Damle.

When Mulk Raj Anand asked me several months ago if I had any more poems collected in English than the one he happened to read in London, I immediately sent him most of the poems I had in hand, as well as several superb English translations from the 1973 *Times Weekly* and some poems that a young Englishman, Graham Smith, had translated for me which were published in Meenakshi Mukherjee's *Vagartha* in 1976. I also have included some poems that two young women, Laurie Hovel and Sylvie Martinez, have been responsible for. They began their translations while on the Associated Colleges of the Midwest programed in Pune, and refined them when they returned to this country to continue their study. But although the selection of poems is mine, it is due to Mulk Raj Anand that this volume has come into being. The field is vast, and constantly growing and changing and I hope many more collections will find their way into the English press.

New language, new experiences, new sources of poetic inspiration, new entrants into a field previously dominated by high castes--these are all non-controversial accomplishments of Dalit Sahitya. There is, however, much controversy. Critics have asked: Can there be Dalit literature, or can there only be literature, regardless of subject ? Can only Dalits write Dalit literature? Can educated ex-Untouchables whose life style is now somewhat middle class be considered Dalit? Those in the Dalit school would say : Yes, there *is* Dalit literature. Only Dalits can write it because only they have experienced the social as well as the economic problems of the lowest of castes. And when educated and no longer poor, they not only remember their childhood, they also suffer from the idea of pollution which remains strong in the Hindu mind, and they identify with their village brothers and sisters who are still subject to outrageous treatment when they claim their full human rights. This volume is full of outrage, but also of hope, of self-criticism as well as criticism of society. My hope is that others will find the poetry as filled with life, as meaningful, as wonderfully and sorrowfully *human* as I do.

Dalit Poetry Translations in English

Hira Bansode. Bosom Friend. Slave. O Great Man. *Phiryad* (complaint, petition.) Pune: Samaj Prabodhan Sanstha Prakashan, 1984.

Pralhad Chendwankar. Empty Advice. Patil. *Audit.* Bombay: Abhinav Prakashan, 1976. "Patil" was first published in English in the *Times Weekly,* (Bombay) November 25, 1973.

Arjun Dangle. Revolution. *Chavni halte ahe* (the cantonment has begun to shake). Bombay: Karmavir Prakashan, 1977. Additional note: many Untouchables worked in the area of the city built for the British army (the cantonment, Marathi: *chavni*) and so the word *chavni* refers to Urban Untouchables living areas.

Namdeo Dhasal. Amber/Sky Alcohols in the Glass. Leaving the House. Their Eternal Pity. *Golpitha* (the name of a slum/prostitutes' area of Bombay). Pune; Nilkanth Prakashan, 1973. First published in English in *Journal of South Asian Literature* XVII:1 (1982). "Now, Now" is also from *Golpitha.*

------ Ambedkar: 1979 and 1980. *Tuhi iyatta kanchi* (what grade are you in?) Bombay: Ambedkar Prabodhini, 1981. "Ambedkar: 1979" was first published in English in *Translation* XXI (Spring 1989). "Ambedkar: 1980" was first published in

Bulletin of Concerned Asian Scholars 23:2 (1991).

------- So That My Mother May be Convinced... *Murkhmhataryane danger halavale* (the old fool who moved mountains.) Pune: Magowa Prakashan, 1975. First published in English in *Bulletin of Concerned Asian Scholars* x:3.

------- Song of the Republic and the Dog. *Golpitha*. Bombay:Nikant Press, 1975. First published in English in *Bulletin of Concerned Asian Scholars* X:3 (1978).

On the way to the Durgah. Poverty as My Own Independent Piece of Land. First published in English in the *Times Weekly* (Bombay) November 25, 1973.

Mina Gajbhiye. Both are Useless. *Asmitadarsh* Diwali issue 1977. The Weeping Wound of Centuries. *Asmitadarsh* Diwali issue 1980.

Anuradha Gaurav, Request. *Asmitadarsh* Diwali issue 1980.

Arun Kamble. Speech. The Life We Live. First published in English in the *Times Weekly* (Bombay) November 25, 1973.

------- Primal Bond. *Vidrohi kavita* (poetry of protest). Edited by Keshav Meshram. Pune: Continental Prakashan, 1978.

Waman Kardak. I Don't Get Angry. *Watcal* (on the

road). Aurangabad: Prabodhan Prakashan, 1972. First published in English in *South Asia Bulletin* VII: 1 and 2 (Fall 1987). *An*

------. In the Darkness Within Me. *Asitadarsh* Jan-Feb-March 1980.

Jyoti Lanjewar. Mother, *Asmitadarsh* Diwali issue 1983.

------ The Nameless One. *Vidrohi kavita*, edited by Keshav Meshram. 2nd expanded edition. Pune: Continental Prakashan, 1987.

Mina Londe. Poem. *Asmitadarsh*. January-February 1988.

Yeshwant Manohar. I'm Ready for Revolt. *Utthangumpha* (the risen cave). Pune: Continental Prakashan, 1980.

Keshav Meshram. One Day I Cursed that Mother-Fucker God. *Vidrohi kavita*. Pune: Continental Prakashan, 1978 First published in English in *Untouchable: Voices of the Dalit Liberation Movement*, edited by Barbara R. Joshi. London: Zed, 1986.

Waman Nimbalkar. Mother. Caste. Words. *Gaokusabaheril kavita* (poetry from beyond the boundary of the Village). Aurangaad: Asmitadarsh Prakashan, 1973; reprinted Nagpur 1979. "Mother" was first published in English in *South*

Asia Bulletin. VII: 1 and 2 (Fall 1987).

Daya Pawar. The Gods of Ocre. Buddha. *Kondwada* (cattle pen). Pune: Magowa Prakashan, 1974. First Published in English in *Journal of South Asian Literature* XVII:I (1982).

------- The City. Vidrohi kavita (poetry of protest). Pune : Continental Prakashan, 1978. First published in English in South Asia Bulletin VII : 1 & 2 (Fall 1987).

------ Four Poems: Hiroshima, Oh Great Poet, You Wrote from Los Angeles, Tree. *Kondwada*. First published in *Vagartha* 12 (1976).

------ Sanskrit (culture). *Kondwada*. Pune: Margowa Prakashan, 1974.

------ Siddharthanagar. *Magowa*. Diwali Issue, 1972. First published in English in *Bulletin of Concerned Asian Scholars* X:3 (1978).

J.V. Pawar. I Have Become the Tide. *Magowa* I: 7-8 (1972). First published in English in *South Asia Bulletin* VII: 1 & 2 (Fall 1987).

------ It's Reddening on the Horizon. *Magowa* I: 7-8 (1978). Naked Mind. Both were first published in English in the *Times Weekly* (Bombay), November 25, 1973.

Tryambak Sapkale. Angulimal, *Surung* (explosion). Aurangabad: Asmitadarsh Prakashan, 1976. First published in English in "Buddhist Sects in Contemporary India" by Eleanor Zelliot *Identity and Division in Cults and Sects in South Asia.* Peter Gaeffke and David A. Utz, editors. Philadelphia: Department of South Asia Regional Studies, 1984.

------ Eklavya ! Do you Want to be a Mother? Day. All three from *Surung.* Aurangabad: Asmitadarsh Prakashan, 1976, and first published in English in *Journal of South Asian Literature* XVII:1 (1982).

Narayan Surve. For I am Brahma. *Aisa ga mi brami!* Bombay: Popular Prakashan, 1976 (1971). First published in this English translation in *The Experience of Hinduism*, edited by Eleanor Zelliot and Maxine Bernsten. Albany: State University of New York Press, 1988.

------ Karl Marx. First published in English in *On the Pavements of Life.* Bombay: Lok Vangmaya Griha, 1973.

Hira Bansode

Hira Bansode-1

BOSOM FRIEND

Today you came over to dinner for the first time
You not only came, you forgot your caste and came
Usually women don't forget that tradition of inequality
But you came with a mind large as the sky to my pocket
size house
I thought you had ripped out all those caste things
You came bridging that chasm that divides us
Truly, friend, I was really happy
With the naive devotion of Shabari I arranged the food
on your plate
But the moment you looked at the plate, your face
changed
With a little smirk you said Oh My--Do you serve chutny-
koshimbir this way?
You still don't know how to serve food
Truly, you folk will never improve

I was ashamed, really ashamed
My hand which had just touched the sky was knocked
down

Hira Bansode 2

I was silent
Toward the end of the meal you asked
What's this? Don't you serve buttermilk or yogurt with the last course of rice?
Oh My Dear, we can't do without that...
The last bit of my courage fell away like a falling star
I was sad, then numb
But the next moment I came back to life
A stone dropped in the water stirs up things on the bottom
So my memories swan up in my mind
Dear Friend--You ask about buttermilk and yogurt
What/How can I tell you?

You know, in my childhood we did't even have milk for tea much less yogurt or buttermilk
My mother cooked on sawdust she brought from the lumberyard wiping away the smoke from her eyes
Every once in a while we might get garlic chutney on coarse bread
Otherwise we just ate bread crumbled in water
Dear Friend-Shrikand was not even a word in our vocabulary
My nose had never smelled the fragrance of

Hira Bansode-3

ghee My tongue had never tasted halva, basundi
Dear Friend--You have not discarded your tradition
Its roots go deep in your mind
And that's true, true, true
Friend--There's yogurt on the last course of rice
Today the arrangement of food on your plate was not properly ordered
Are you going to tell me what mistakes I made?
Are you going to tell me my mistakes?

Translated by Jayant Karve and Eleanor Zelliot

Hira Bansode-4

SLAVE

Where the doors are decorated with mango leaves
Where the houses are ornamented with little flaming oil
lamps
In that country a woman is still a slave

Where Sita entered the fire to prove her fidelity
Where Ahilya was turned to stone because of Indra's lust
Where Draupadi was fractured to serve five husbands
In that country a woman is still a slave

Where a woman's identity fades like nature's blossoms
Where delicate jewels of emotion are trampled under
a heel
Where the free birds of dreams are scorned
In that country a woman is still a slave

Where the sky-flowers of desire must be left to float
down the river

Hira Bansode-5

Where the threatening force of women's mind must be buried in the earth
Where the silvery moonlight of happiness must be poured into a jar of darkness
In that country a woman is still a slave
Where a woman in her youth is dried up by Tradition she is confined all her life like a stunted tree she remains in the shadow of someone else's light
In that country a woman is still a slave

In that country where women are still slaves the conflagration starts in the hours made of flowers
The festival of lordship is celebrated with joy but the stories of all that are recited with pain

To be born a woman is unjust
To be born a woman is unjust

Translated by S.K. Throat and Eleanor Zelliot

Hira Bansode-6

O GREAT MAN

O Great Man
Those who strewed thorns in your path
today offer you flowers
and sing your praises
--now this is really too much--

During the dark procession of time
you lit the flowers of light
but these imposters, these villains
crushed, extinguished those flowers.
Today those flowers have turned into a wildfire
and those villains are fanning that wildfire
--oh now this is too much--

Like an elephant ramming a gate
you pounded on the temple door,
the stones of the temple shook.
Under the holy name of religion
they long ago enslaved the gods.
Your honest painful claim

Hira Bansode-7

of the right to see the gods
was crushed, thrown out of the village.
Now they decorate the great tree
that sprouted on that spot
-now this is really too much-

It is clear that nature belongs to all
but these people bought that too.
Every drop of water in Chawdar Tank
was stamped with their name,
the alert watchman of this culture
guarded the imprisoned water.
They feared that your touch
would poison the water and
they annointed you with your blood
when you were dying of thirst.
And now they pour water
into the mouth of your stone effigy
--oh now this is too much--

Translated by Jayant Karve and Eleanor Zelliot

Note: Chawdar Tank is the pond in Mahad which ws the center of riot in 1927 when Untouchabkes eed by Dr. B.R. Ambedkar attempted to drink its water. A satyagraha and the burning of the Brahman law book Manusmriti took place at Mahad in the following months.

Pralhad Chéndwankar

Pralhad Chendwankar-1

EMPTY ADVICE

This country which demands
a pot of blood
for a swallow of water-
How can I call it mine
though it give the world
the (empty) advice of peace?

Translated by Jayashree Godhale-Turner

Pralhad Chenwankar-2

PATIL

When Patil sent
for me, I went
"Sitdown," he said, yet
ground was wet.

Threw at my head
torn sacking jute
still there I stood
quite mute.

Patil cracked betelnut
yelled, "Why ain't this runt
bloody scum dancing on boards
to fill its gut?"

Paunch-scratching, spewed
forth filth-abuse.
I went on standing mute
rooted still within my boots.

Wonder now, why did I stand?

Pralhad Chenwankar-3

Hadn't eaten no fodder
at his father's hand.

Translated by Gauri Deshpande

Arjun Dangle

Arjun Dangle-1

REVOLUTION

We used to be their friends
when, clay pots hung from our necks,
brooms tied to our rumps,
we made our rounds through the Upper Lane
calling "Ma-bap, Johar, Ma-bap"

We fought with crows,
never even giving them the snot from our noses
as we dragged out the Upper Lane's dead cattle,
skinned it neatly
and shared the meat among ourselves.
They used to love us then.
We warred with jackals-dogs-vultures-kites
because we ate their share.

Today we see a root-to-crown change.
Crows-jackals-dog-vultures-kites
are our closest friends.
The Upper Lane doors are closed to us.

Arjun Dangle-2

"Shout victory to the Revolution
"Shout victory"

"Burn, burn those who strike at tradition."

Translated by Jayant Karve and Eleanor Zelliot

Translators' notes: In the Peshwa days of the 18th century, according to legend. untouchables wore pots around their necks to keep their spittle from polluting the ground and brooms to obliterate their footprints. The Mahar used a special greeting. "Johar, Ma-bap" (hail, mother and father), rather than the usual "Ram Ram" or "Namaste," and among his traditional duties was the hauling of cattle carcasses from the village. The final verse is ironic, not exhortative. "Shout victory to the Revolution" is a quotation from a Brahman poet. Dangle's point is that while the elite call for revolution, those who revolt are burned.

Namdeo Dhasal

Namdeo Dhasal-1

AMBER/SKY ALCOHOLS IN THE GLASS

My everything amber/sky alcohols in the glass
let breath reel stagger
"lover
I swear I don't get love"
Let snake-veins keep the beat move shake
the raga of gutter-ganges
Let the donkey under your skin bray
Let flow the pain, the dark serpent, the charging boar
let your balls sizzle
an honest beast in your torch
now is yours
Sell cheap faith-in-Christ, family-plan your vulgarity
kick this heavenly virtue, this fatherly atrocity
this poor promising puking lamb
Crumpled-paper-Pandurang-dindi goes on singing
winding
the sweet notes flute
Juhu beach fragranced
a quarter jingle jangles
daughters wed between their thighs

Namdeo Dhasal-2

Uncle Uncle Little Star
Strumming
the delicate guitar of impurity
Listen to the dainty ankle bells
Your future is yours alone
police : pot belly : much around : a thousand days' night

count every yard everything's hard
Bitter fate
O Allah cork the bottle
A Allah fit a loop
the sin of your Diwali
itches a lot
silly malang raise the palang
the chillum is sticky the hands-feet are numb
fix a dose : play hide and seek
let's roll and rub like Mira
chutney
ghutney
the share depends on the size of the brood
ungrateful bastard
breast-breaking auntie
in what situation did you drop your calf
fabrics itch
your mate

Namdeo Dhasal-3

abraca dabraca
skeleton in petticoat
prayers to himself for his own realm. That's allowed
the full glass vomits fragrance
grance
muck
in dreams
in liquor
in the glass
come come come come God
    crush the frogs in the earthenware pot
    blow out the lamp
    of the umpteen generations
    suck, drool over the pelvic bone
    My essence droops drunken
    why pull it up
For everyone in front of everyone the wine filled glass.

Translated by Jayant Karve and Eleanor Zelliot with the assistance of A.K. Ramanujan

Translators' notes : Dhasal uses the Sanskrit word for sky, ambar, and seems to be clearly making a play on the English word, amber, the color of alcohol. He makes a verb of the Marathi noun for alcohol, which is an ungrammatical in Marathi as it is in English. The quoted line is from a Hindi film song. Pandurang-dindi refers to the pilgrimage to Pandharpur, an important religious event in Maharashtra. Malang is a Muslim holy man; palang is a bed. Mira is a Rajput princess and saint-poet.

Namdeo Dhasal-4

LEAVING THE HOUSE

As you leave the house, the doors should be left as they are.
We have avatared
to cover your white forehead with kum kum.
Tell me I'm yours. Say I'm yours.
Why don't you say somethin'? Why don't you say somethin'?
Look, we've brought this brand new slate with us.
Gimme an answer : answer me; give, I say.
Prostitutes multiply:
question mark question mark question mark
Slums multiply : question mark question mark question mark
Hunger deaths multiply:
question mark question mark question mark
Beggars multiply: question mark question mark question mark
Men without work multiply:

Namdeo Dhasal-5

question mark question mark
question mark

Why do questions multiply, multiply: questions:
Why wasteland: why more wasteland?
You are silent
You will be given only three minutes

speak
speak speak
speak speak speak

O.K.
We're turning our backs on you right now.
Right now we're becoming assassins
taking off even the doors as we leave,
running war-tanks over you
Spit on you; I Sit on you: Spit! Spit! Sky Us. Sky. Us.

Translated by Jayant Karve and Eleanor Zelliot

Namdeo Dhasal-6

THEIR ETERNAL PITY

Their eternal pity--no taller than the pimp on Falkland Road.
No pavillion put up in the sky for us.
Lords of wealth, they are, locking up light in those vaults of theirs
In this life, carried by a whore, not even the sidewalks are ours
Made so beggarly it is nausea to be human,
cannot fill our shrivelled gut even with dirt.
Each new just day supports them as if bribed--
    not a sigh slips through the fingers of day's plenty
    as we are cut down.

Translated by Jayant Karve and Eleanor Zelliot

Namdeo Dhasal-7

NOW, NOW

Turning their backs to the sun, they journeyed through
centuries;
Now, now, we must refuse to be pilgrims of darkness.
    That one, our father, is bent from carrying,
    carrying and darkness.Now, now we must lift that
    burden from his back.
Our blood was spilled for this glorious city
And what we got to eat was the right to eat stones.
Now, now, we must explode that building which kisses
the

sky!
After a thousand years we were blessed with a
sunflower-giving *fakir;*
Now, now, we must, like sunflowers, turn our faces to the
sun.

Translated by Jayant Karve and Eleanor Zelliot

Translators' note: The reference is clearly to Ambedkar, and the connotation of fakir seems to be miracle-worker.

Namdeo Dhasal-8

AMBEDKAR : 79

Your followers act like false gurus
They use a loincloth for a tie and babble
Their heritage is mother-fucking
Like Yama fucked Yami, they fuck their sisters
These impotent Arjuns of countless generations--
all they can do is pop some virgin's cherry,
    the sun in their blood
This bubbling mass
who will pop it with a pin?
This sad lonesome rain, where is it going?
Won't somebody set this city on fire?

Your death is considered monumental
I saw it from the eyes of a common man
There was no joy in your death, no sorrow
The real man lives before death
The rest is simply dust, swirling dust
In place of death I'm trying to establish
    Beauty.
This is the proclamation of bread
This is the parliament's brothel
This country we call Mother
sleeps with the god of wealth
and time is becoming more orthodox

Namdeo Dhasal-9

The life in my heart become worthless as dust
Green dreams fade before my eyes
Now who can we worship?

Translated by Laurie Hovell and Asha Mundlay, with Jayant Karve

Namdeo Dhasal-10

AMBEDKAR : 1980

1.

You died, but didn't cease to be.
Like us, you slept with your wife
You brought forth children, but didn't let them flap in the wind
While we grew up like this, like that, somehow, anyhow.
But our children
Will never dare deny your affection
Academician/technician/politician/scientist/philosopher
These men will define you any which way

But you lived like a man
There was no acting in it
No dramatics
No imitation, no imitators

Now this is old stuff,
That they wouldn't touch us when they gave us water
Now this is old stuff,
That they made us sit outside the school on the veranda

Namdeo Dhasal-11

Now this is old
That they wouldn't let us see
The black and white feet of the god Vithoba
Now they and we are all alike
This world's socialism

This world's *communism*
And all those things of theirs
We've put them to the test
And the implication is this
Our shadow can cover our feet

2.
I 've cursed you too, but
you gave us the tongue to curse
I've even sunk you in the water, but
you gave us the water.
We've done things to you, even so,
anything can be done to you
But the question of my loyalty,
my honesty
still remains.
Who are you?
Who were you?
Whose are you?

Namdeo Dhasal-12

3.

The times are wholly yours
but your people still suffer
A mendicant can be Prime Minister here
but not a Mang or a Bhangi.
In front of the chair, the parliament's value is less
In front of the law, the prostitute's value is less
One thing I saw in all this
the wheel of seasons came to us equally
you like the wheel were equal to all.

4.

It was a Friday
An arithmetic book, a slate,
and one piece of chalk
mother, eager, brought from the bazaar.
She was very tired that day
In the light of the brass lantern
she made me massage her hands and feet
Then she said,
"Baba-until I fall asleep
Take a look at this book.
I never learned
but you do this.
To start your education

make B for Babasaheb.
He was far more beautiful than Lord Ganesh.
So don't trace
Shri Ganesh.
The lord of the people is never ugly
He comes from among men
True/Holy/Beautiful
Babasaheb Ambedkar
is true, holy, beautiful
Otherwise this book has no meaning.

5.

While I was writing this
three O'clock struck
though I want to have a drink
I don't feel like drinking.
I only want to sleep peacefully
and tomorrow see no varnas, no castes.

Translated by Asha Mundlay and Laurie Hovell, with Jayant Karve and Eleanor Zelliot

Translators' notes : Underlined words are originally in English. "Our shadow can cover our feet"-Untouchables were not allowed in the caste Hindu part of the village at times of the day when their shadow could pollute. Mang and Bhangi are Untouchable castes. A Maharashtrian child traditionally writes "Shri Ganesh" at the top of his writing tablet; Dhasal's mother asked him to write B for Babasahab Ambedkar instead. The concluding word of the poem, varna, means colour and/or the classic division of people into four "caste" divisions.

Namdeo Dhasal-14

SO THAT MY MOTHER MAY BE CONVINCED...

A body broken down for seven generations
Gentle mother, your feet haven't travelled through the ten continents,
You never, never, never could leave your village world.

Throughout your life you carried, with your eyes shut, the burden of Devout Wife.
With no other way, you read again and again the stones and boulders.
Without speaking, you took the heirloom mantle of Chaste wife.
You wore the long, long robes of the Married Woman.
All your life, you have put patches on your heart,
on your pride in living, on the clothes on your body,
on your home.
In your prime, you became weak, naive, a tethered cow.
Mother, you never understood:
this land does not value the woman, the Shudra, the worker, the landless.

Namdeo Dhasal-15

Today your son, in his twenties, stumble-shuffling, of
whom you made an elephant from a grain of sand
enduring the hot winds of poverty and hard times,
whom you fed grains of rice while your own stomach
pinched,
whom you nurtured, making a lamp of your eyes and a
cradle of your arms

whom you protected in the stress of life as one protects
a sore on the palm of the Land,
Mother, he, your favourite, has rebelled against this
culture,this
tradition, this custom, this thought and these justifiers
of the status quo.

Now, you are exhausted, shaken
You cry instead of placing a helmet on my head.
Mother, all that is unnecessary.
Mother, your son is not a child.
He is the son of this age's rebellion.
He can see clearly the injustice, himself as victim.
Governmental machinery, means of living, power of toll,
mines of coal and steel, warehouses, factories,
there: protection, guarantee of food and money.
My face, lying in the dust, separated from all of this.

Namdeo Dhasal-16

Mother, as your ancestors have not given you anything,
so you have not given me anything
You haven't taught me the wise ways of history.
Father has drunk the liquor of this system and is intoxicated.
Mother, you have drunk the water of ignorance and are finished.
Like an ordinary woman, you dream of a son's married life.
In your mind you have a grandson, plump as the child
        on the Amul milk tin,
        a one-in-a-million daughter-in-law
        a little bird's house, with you
        looking after everything with your old eyes.
In your petty-petty mind, resounding kisses and overflowing love.
In the end, a peaceful death,
        while you still wear kum kum in never-ending bliss.
Mother, remember your troubled life.
The start of your life-
that day you were a new bride, anointed with tumeric,

brought ceremoniously to your father-in-law's house.
How many wishes, how many hopes, were in your mind.
From this to now-dragged through life.
Mother, doesn't it gnaw you?

How can you so easily drop a curtain
over the atrocities of those long years?
Can you tell me the purpose, the reasons, for your suffering?
All your life you were sucked dry and even now you bow before the system.
Your natural fearlessness, your willing drudgery,
your ability to make decisions,
your wanting to learn new techniques of production,
your prominent place in individual development, public development,
your faith in freedom, your part in national defence,
your accomplishments in all of this,
all of this vanished when man came to know the use of land.
The male-dominated culture kept you withering in kitchen

and children, gave you secondary status.
You were seen as machinery for the production of worms.
Your natural being, your gift of giving colour to masculinity,
fell into slavery.
Mother, your woman's life story lives in a house in my
heart.
It makes me see you clearly.
That's why I don't kill you, don't strip out your innards
Because-just as I have been stripped bare, so have you.
I want to rip out his innards.
At this moment. mother, I need you.
Please understand me.

Mother, we are separated from our origins,
and all people like us have lost their identity.
The circumstances which brought these days to you,
me, father, all of us,-
Mother, I want control over those circumstances.
Long before we can effectively confront our enemy, you
must trust me.
I am going through all this for happiness and a high
standard of living.

Namdeo Dhasal-19

O mother of poverty, don't think my hardship is trivial.
Look, poverty's at the door.
Don't come in my way with love and affection.
Don't forecast defeat for the weapon which the 20th century has put in your sons's hands.
A weapon increases respectibility!
We had no history. A weapon will create history!
Mother, I don't need your love and barren affection.
I need your faith, I need your sacrifice.

Mother, we don't have any right to even this petty, simple life.
I need the payment money to get those rights.
Mother, today, tell me the stories of that payment.
In the 18th century the whole human race was turned upside down.
but even today you haven't heard of it.
You don't know the chronology of the buying and selling of humans.
You don't know the nations and the John Hawkinses who traded in slaves.
You don't know that on 21st January 1793 the guillotine was raised and before thousands of people Louis XVI was beheaded.

Namdeo Dhasal-20

You don't know the terrible massacre in history,
don't know the revolutionary year of 1948,
don't know Bebeuf who brought the torch of liberty.

Mother, the day that you cut my umbilical cord, why
didn't you slash my throat with your fingernail?
Today you are terrified just thinking of my torment,
terrified of my imprisonment, the future noose.

Mother, I can't tolerate this cool death.
Please understand all this.
The 20th century has given eyes to your son;
he will lead you on the path of plenty.
Even if he falls on the battlefield, say with pride,
"He was mine."
He will create wise economists,
he will re-shape the land,
he will produce the things that the people need.
You yourself used to say, "O Lord, give me a strong son
Who will put his banner on top of the three worlds."
Mother, think of me like that.
Mother, you have been sucked dry all your life.

Namdeo Dhasal-21

You didn't even moo once from the depths.
You didn't stir the sky with a shrill cry.
The earth didn't crack.
How easily you lived, wrapped in rhinoceros hide.
Mother, I cannot put on the hide of a rhinoceros.
I have been aware of the exploitation and I have lost myself.
The bliss of life in blinkers!
I have become Satan.
When I see women selling their bodies or begging in the bazaar,
Mother, I think of you.
Mother, what has this country given to you,
this country which teaches begging and incest.
Mother, be the support for my weapon.

O mother of poverty, make me free for the new world.
You have become bent thinking of my execution.
If you crumble to dust at this crucial moment,
then I'll have to walk on over your inert body.
Mother, please don't make me master of that deed.

Translated by Jayant Karve, Vidyut Bhagwat and Eleanor Zelliot

Translators' Note : This early poem of Dhasal's is trite at times, bombastic and doctrinaire at others, but has been included because of its power and its shocking difference from the traditional sentimental Marathi "mother" poem.

Namdeo Dhasal-22

SONG OF THE REPUBLIC AND THE DOG

Dog, leashed dog,
He howls and barks from time to time
This is his constitutional right.
He lives on stale crumbs.
His mind is calloused with endured injustice.
If at a rebellious moment it becomes unbearable and he
jerks at his leash, tries to break his chain then he is shot.

In the crowded streets
the drums of bunkus freedom are played.
Friends, I ask an uncircumcised boy
the meaning of democracy.
"What do you eat with it?"
I ask the mother with the wornout old patched sari
the worth of breast milk.
I ask the man who works like an ox
about fulfilment, prosperity, deprivation.
These riddles have turned my mind helter-shelter
"Red carriage with green handles widowed prostitutes
sit inside"

Namdeo Dhasal-23

Do you know, do you know what it is?

He whose heart has become stone
and his skin a rhinoceros hide
and he is hanging stuffed with sawdust in a museum
now only his head can remain
cool, cool, expansive and peaceful.
How terrible, how terrible the age is,
the thieves' age.
We can't even chat about crops and water.
The dark empire of hunger, the guts which have run dry,
the ferocious python which wanders in them
--and we are not even allowed to weep.
Liberty, equality, fraternity,
the banyan tree of private property---
everything is equal before the law.
"Eat, drink and be merry Go to hell."
O how strange is this age, this dark age.
We live to drink tea in cafes.
We touch cup to cup, saucer to saucer.
We search the railway timetable for a two-hour journey.
We try to fill up the Kumbhamela of our existence
with many colours and fashions.

Namdeo Dhasal-24

After great tension we gather in public gardens.
We play a rhythmic flute of our breaths.
The two children of poverty,
One white, one black.
Sea-saws are played on in sovereign gardens.
Dry tombs are impressed on the screen of the mind.
The laundatory songs of democracy are forced down.
Hybrid, hybrid--
what bastard brought this to us?
It won't take root in flesh
It won't mix in blood
It won't flower or give fruit
It won't give shade to the weary and tired
It no more fits the body than a ready-made shirt.
The gaping wounds on the body will not vanish.
We are becoming homeless.

We are becoming orphans.
Leaving our houses to the winds we are returning to the burial grounds.
We dig up the bones of forty-two generations.
We sell them for four annas a kilo.
We fill the belly of the skeleton.
In the nation which spewed "golden smoke"

Namdeo Dhasal-25

the marketplace of bones is flourishing.

We have become fakirs of fate.
Golden sparrow, golden sparrow
golden birdseed, golden cage.
We are being sold.
How nice are these travellers
How nice are these beggars.
How nice are these hunters.
In their hands the white hunted rabbits.
On the table spread with a nice cloth they have placed their prey.
They pull out the dagger--swish, swish---
they pierce the rabbit's genitals
The geyser of blood gushes forth.

My mind is turning into blood-bathed doves.
The messengers of peace are dashing along the path of the sky.
The song emerges from the chaos, the song of the Republic:
"Give alms, the eclipse is over.
Give alms, the eclipse is over.

Translated by Vidya Dixit, Gail Omvedt, Jayant Karve, Bharat Patankar and Eleanor Zelliot

Translators' Notes: The answer to the Marathi proverb is "watermelon." The final couplet is the chant of the Untouchable who traditionally begged after an eclipse was over.

Namdeo Dhasal-26

ON THE WAY TO THE DURGAH

The leaking sun

Went out
In the embrace of the night
When I was born
On the pavement
In the rags
An instant orphan---

The woman who delivered me
Went to the father in heaven
For she could not stand the
Vampires of the pavement
And needed to wash her sari
Clean of the stains of darkness
And like a man whose fuse
Has been blown
I grew up nourished by roadside shit
Saying, "Give me five cents
I'll give you Five punches"
On the way to the Durgah.

Translated by Dilip Chitre

Editors' Note: A durgah is the tomb of a Muslim holy man whose power to aid supplicants remains in his tomb after his death.

Namdeo Dhasal-27

POVERTY AS MY OWN INDEPENDENT PIECE OF LAND

Destiny willing, the form may change or may not.
Even then poverty itself is my own independent piece of land
And as I cultivate it my days rise
And my days fall...
Earlier men could have been the wretched slaves of the soil
I refused to make compromises with the later feudal lords
My limbs of a forest were fostered by geometric contagion
Drenched me in gentle is innocence
I am the headless body of a rat with a pyramid rising above me
Meat and fish
Rice and eggs
Bootleg liquor and the flowers of white champak
Kisses, embraces, coital postures, jewels
And beds, and a house with a leaking roof,
And the rhythm of a lullaby.

Namdeo Dhasal-28

I am squeezed: in my yearning
Feminine beauty flowers
The Mona Lisa painted by Leonardo da Vinci
In the service of A-B
Rain driving down in sheets, a dying cigarette,
A dehydrated dancing girl
Contrasting colour harmony
I too have poverty as my own independent piece of land...

Translated by Dilip Chitre

Mińa Gaybhiye

Mina Gajbhiye-1

THE WEEPING WOUND OF CENTURIES

I had sutured with difficulty
        the weeping wound of centuries
Those stitches are all ripped out, ripped out by Marathwada
Even our old bonds of give and take are snapped
From now on I won't scream "I want to live"
From now on I'll live to die

Let the village become a burning ground
        along with me
I will not live like a dog, nowhere

Note : Marathwada: There were massive riots in 1978 over the proposal to re-name Marathwada University after Dr. B.R. Ambedkar, the Untouchable leader who had brought higher education to the area. The violence cost several lives and much loss of Dalit and Buddhist homes and property in the Marathwada area.

Mina Gajbhiye-2

BOTH ARE USELESS

What will you do for those
whose hunger is an ache?
Shed two tears?
Give a fourth of a slice of bread?
What will you do for those
who don't quite live
and don't quite die?
Write a beautiful poem on life?
Or a beautiful poem on death?
What ever you do--
It'll be useless.

Translated by Jayant Karve and Eleanor Zelliot

Anuradha Gaurav

Anuradha Gaurav-1

REQUEST

We give our children to the God Khandoba,
Offer them to Yellama, Shantadurga
        of our own will!
We make our daughters lie beneath men!
We mother-fuckers like dumb beasts
        hock our lives.
We know what's going wrong
But what can we do?
Our ancestors did the same thing
        we are doing today
Our children will inherit that same thing.
When there was Ramraj on earth
Rama used his sword against Shambak!
Our eyes were shut then, too.

Oh we do plead with you
        don't let those tears flow for us
Oh, hands clasped, we beg of you
        don't be the least distressed on our behalf
Don't wash the stinking rags of our lives--

Anuradha Gaurav-2

one day each year!
We are naked already.
Don't strip us in front of the whole world.

Translated by Sylvie Martinez, S.K. and Vimal Throat and Eleanor Zelliot

Note : Untouchables traditionally have been among the chief donors of children to serve various gods and goddesses, with the result that many become prostitutes The reference to Rama is from the Ramayana, in which Ram killed a Shudra for listening to the Vedas.

Arun Kamble

Arun Kamble-1

SPEECH

Bone-chewing granpus
at burning ghat
permanent resident
of my heart
with weight of tradition
behind his back
yells, "Sadding bastard, I
tell you,,
stutter with *our* tongue!"

Picking through the Vedas
buttering his queue
Brahman teacher at school
bellows, "Speak *my* pure tongue,
whoreson!"

Now, you tell me, which speech
am I to tongue?

Translated by Gauri Deshpande

Arun Kamble-2

THE LIFE WE LIVE

If you were to live the life we live
then out of you would poems arise.
We: kicked and spat at for our piece of bread.
You: fetch fulfillment and name of the Lord.
We: down-gutter degraders of our heritage.
You: its sole repository, descendants of the sage
We: never have a paisa to scratch our arse.
You: the golden cup of offerings in your bank.
Your bodies flame in sandalwood
ours are shoved under half-turned sand.
Wouldn't the world change, and fast
if you were forced to live at last
this life that's all we've always had?

Translated by Gauri Deshpande

Arun Karnble-3

PRIMAL BOND

From what generation to what generation
is this journey?
And I am like this:
when I contain all brightness and all darkness
why do I bear this dead skin,
these sighs?

From under what seer's beard
came this insomnia,
this hypnotic coma

embracing Tme?
And this face of mine, found in an excavation
is faithful to what connection?

.... and this flock of white swams
flying up in the sky
this burning vinyard of skinless grapes
what place should be set afire?
In what kitchen was this body made-
a "pure" one?
and this flock of white swans...
All this as if fused together.

How much of this romantic nonsense:

Arun Kamble-4

"...I want to paint your picture
I want to sing you a poem
I want to fill my eyes with you
I want to marry you."

Go on walking around with sun flowers
and then quench their sun faces.
You are from that ageless tradition.
But how can I call you a poison girl?
Why are you faithful to
that skeleton found in an excavation?

Turn your dust smeared face this way
and salvage these lives.
A stone lying in the bazaar.

I don't know why, girl,
but I see in you an ancient skeleton
thousands of years old,
found in an excavation...

The primal bond of the universe

Arun Kamble-5

which blesses the phenomenon
of procreation
is forming in you.

Translated by Jayant Karve and Eleanor Zelliot

Translators' Notes : Poison girl refers to an ancient story of women who were fed poison slowly until they could kill anyone who slept with them while tolerating the poison themselves. Stone in the bazaar refers to the classical story of Ahilya, turned to stone by a curse and awakening only to the touch of Rama's foot. The translators' interpretation of this poem is that it is addressed to a Brahman girl who represents traditional India.

Waman Kardak

Waman Kardak-1

I DON'T GET ANGRY

I don't get angry; this is my sin.
Who can I blame, tell me, who can I blame?

The village is the same, the villagers are the same.
When my Bhim was alive, they used to tremble.
King Bhim went away, cowardice came.

Even though I met with cruel hard times
Bhim was with me, my head was held high.
But today I have diminished the Bhim in me.

Here, there, they strip naked my mothers, my sisters.
I don't get angry, I don't get angry
Today I see my own honour dishonoured.

My own daughter's virtue is looted in public,
my eyes look on, my body shakes,
cowardice grows from my helplessness.

My brother is burned alive in my hut.
What happened, what did not, doesn't go in the book.

Waman Kardak-2

Today I myself wipe out the marks my feet have made.

Every day the axe falls on my people.
My hunger, my dead will, are guests in my house.
I am cowed and that doubles the torment.

I was a lion's cub, now I'm a lamb's tail.
The people are wolves; who'll hunt the wolves?
My blood does not boil like King Bhim's did.

A new Peshwa has come, grinding me underfoot.
I don't get angry, I don't get angry.
With my own hands, I 've burnt my everything to ash.

Translated by Jayant Karve and Eleanor Zelliot

Translators' Note : This song of a popular Dalit folk singer recalls the days of the active movement under the leadership of Dr. Bhimrao Ramji Ambedkar (Bhim.) The Peshwai refers to the 18th century rule of the Brahman Prime Ministers of Maharashtra.

Waman Kardak-3

IN THE DARKNESS WITHIN ME

Opening my eyes wide
I search in the dark within me
until my eyeballs are seared.
A poet sees what the sun cannot, they say,
but the little lamp of creativity wouldn't kindle.
Some go around lighting one light from another, they say
but who'd come to a village drowned in darkness?
Looks like someone covered over the sun,
the full moon, the moonlight too.
Did someone swallow the sky?

A sonorous voice I think is mine
rings insistently in my ears:
    Become the fuse of a dynamite charge.
    Blast the darkness to pieces.
    In you are the waters, the light, the winds.
    Free them.
    Go to the sky. Become a cloud. Make rain.
    Quench earth's thirst.
    Become a glittering star. Give light to the earth.
    Ride the wind.

Waman Kardak-4

Chase away the army of darkness.
Search the sky, The moon, the sun, the stars.
The light is in you.
The light is in you.
Be tomorrow's sun.

Translated by Jayant Karve and Eleanor Zelliot

Jyoti Lanjewar

Jyoti Lanjewar-1

MOTHER

I have never seen you
wearing one of those gold-bordered saris
with a gold necklace
with gold bangles
with fancy sandals.
Mother! I have seen you
burning the soles of your feet in the harsh summer sun
hanging your little ones in a cradle on an acacia tree
carrying barrels of tar
working on a road cunstruction crew...

I have seen you
with a basket of earth on your head
rags bound on your feet
giving a sweaty kiss to the naked child
who came tottering over to you,
working for your daily wage, working, working...

I have seen you
turning back the tide of tears
trying to ignore your stomach's growl

Jyoti Lanjewar-2

suffering parched throat and lips
building a dam on a lake...

I have seen you
for a dream of four mud walls
stepping carefully, pregnant,
on the scaffolding of a sky scraper
carrying a hod of wet cement on your head...

I have seen you
evenings, untying the end of your sari

for the coins to buy salt and oil,
putting a five-paise coin
on a little hand
saying "go eat candy"
taking the little bundle from the cradle to your breast
saying "Study, become an Ambedkar
and let the baskets fall from my hands"...

I have seen you
sitting in front of the stove
burning your very bones
to make coarse bread and a little something

Jyoti Lanjewar-3

to feed everybody, but half-fed yourself
so there'd be a bit in the morning...

I have seen you
washing clothes and cleaning pots
in different households
rejecting the scraps of food offered to you
with pride
covering yourself with a sari
that had been mended so many time
saying, "Don't you have a mother or a sister?"
to anyone who looked at you with lust in his eyes...

I have seen you
on a crowded street with a market basket on your head
trying always to keep your head covered with the end of
your sari
chasing anyone who nudged you deliberately
with your sandal in your hand...

I have seen you working until sunset
piercing the darkness to turn toward home,
then forcing from the door
that man who staggered in from the hooch hut...

Jyoti Lanjewar-4

I have seen you
at the front of the Long March
the end of your sari tucked tightly at the waist
shouting "Change the name,"
taking the blow of the police stick on your upraised hands
going to jail with head held high...

I have seen you
saying when your only son
fell martyr to police bullets
"you died for Bhim, your death means something"
saying boldly to the police
"If I had two or three sons, I would be fortunate.
They would fight on."

I have seen you
on your death bed
giving that money you earned
rag-picking to the *diksha bhumi*
saying with your dying breath
"Live in unity...fight for Baba...don't forget him..."
and with your very last breath
"Jai Bhim"

Jyoti Lanjewar-5

I have seen you...
I have never seen you
ever wanting a new broad-bordered sari

Mother, I have seen you...

Translated by Sylvie Martinez, S.K Vimal Thorat and Eleanor Zelliot.

Translators' Notes : The long March took place in March 1979 after a governmental decision to rename Marathawada University in honour of Dr. Babasaheb B.R. Ambedkar was reversed. Other references to the Ambedkar movement occur in the next two stanzas. "You died for Bhim" uses the affectionate shortening of Bhimrao Ramji Ambedkar's first name; the reference is to the Marathawada Riots, the Worli Riots or some other conflict in which Dalits were killed. The dikshá bhumi is the site of the conversion to Buddhism in 1956 in Nagpur. Baba is another common and affectionate nickname for Babasaheb Ambedkar. Jyoti Lanjewar's entire poem is a pain of praise to the hard working dalit women who in spite of illiteracy and many forms of back-breaking labour give great dedication and strength to the dalit movement begun by Ambedkar.

Jyoti Lanjewar-6

THE NAMELESS ONES

Begging won't get anything here
not sympathy, not love,
A suit in court wins injustice,
Tears are of no value,
Getting water is a struggle,
Wrapping yourself in smoke from a dead fire won't work,
You have to plant the cinder of revolt in your own body
At times there is a firefly of revolt flickering--may be counterfeited
But at those times give it outside air to see if it glows.

"The revolution will come through poetry."
Once I accepted that.
But poetry does not live by making revolution.
The same faithless faces of yesterday
extend the hand of friendship
while wondering with a sword...and
in their struggle with the enemy were made impotent.
They burned houses down with words
But after the house burned, the words died.

Jyoti Lanjewar-7

For the sake of the poetry of humanity
    one must be so very human,
But they change direction with the wind...
And these green parrots of the dry desert turn out to be a mirage.
They turn their eyes where they wish, according to their own convenience.

When there is no strength
in their own wings

They find the convenient words
to cut the wings of others.

They make palaces of words!
But I have seen them crumble.
"Kala Ram" and "Chawdar Tank"--

    the history of pain
    is carved on each of our hearts.
But even if they could carve words on water
    The Indrayani will not save them.

Translated by S.K. and Vimal Thorat and Eleanor Zelliot

Note : This poem is about those current leaders and poets of the Dalits who have, in Jyoti Lanjewar's eyes, betrayed the movement.

Jyoti Lanjewar-8

In the last stanza of the poem, "Kala Ram" and "Chawdar Tank" refer to two great events in the movement led by Dr. B.R. Ambedkar: the 1930-1935 satyagraha at the Kala Ram Temple at Nasik for temple entry, and the 1928-1929 struggle at Chawdar Tank in Mahad for the right to drink from a public water supply - two events which are symbolic of the power of Ambedkar's leadership, offered as a contrast to the leaders of today whose words are not built upon action and manuski am- true humanity. The last line refers to the devotional poetry of the seventeenth century saint Tukaram, which had to be cast into the Indrayani River on the order of the Brahmans, but which the Indrani saved and returned miraculously to Tukaram (and the people of Maharashtra.)

Mina Londe

Mina Londe-1

POEM

Don't look at me as if *you* were an orphan.
We are more than refugees
    without homes here
    a burden of centuries on our backs
    and even with that no footprints
    on this muddy piece of land
If the earth is not ours
How can we speak of the sky?

Translated by S.K. Thorat and Elea

Yeshwant Manohar

Yeshwant Manohar-1

I'M READY FOR REVOLT

I'm burning with a feeling of revolt
        and I call out to you
I will write the poem of revolt on your sword
Today I have become a storm-come with me!
I reach out to you-give me your hand!
I have become the sun, my friend--sing with me!
I have become the fire, today I am afire with fire-
        give voice to the volcano within *you*!

I'm out of my senses, out of control
Make me a limitless sky with words
I will hurl myself into the battle
If I should win, shout out my victory!
If I should break, bury me deep!
If I come to your door confused, try to understand me!
If I return bloodied, hold me to your breast!
If I die out there, take my body in your arms!
Someone make me believe I am and will be yours!
Shed a few tears and remember me forever!

Translated by S.K. and Vimal Thorat and Eleanor Zelliot

Keshav Meshram

Keshav Meshram-1

ONE DAY I CURSED THAT MOTHER-FUCKER GOD

One day I cursed that mother-fucker God.
He just laughed shamelessly.
My neighbour-a born-to-the-pen Brahman--was shocked.
He looked at me with his castor-oil face and said,
"How can you say such things to the
source of the Indescribable,
Qualityless, Formless Juggernaut?
Shame on you for trying to catch his dharma-hood
in a noose of words."

I cursed another good hot curse.
The university buildings shuddered and sank waist-deep.
All at once, scholars began doing research
into what makes people angry.
They sat in their big rooms fragrant with incense,
their bellies full of food,
and debated.

On my birthday, I cursed God.

Keshav Meshram-2

I cursed him, I cursed him again.
Whipping him with words, I said
"Bastard!
"Would you chop a whole cart of wood
for a single piece of bread?
"Would you wipe the sweat from your bony body
with your mother's ragged sari?
"Would you wear out your brothers and sisters
for your father's fix?
"Would you work as a pimp
to keep him in booze?

"Oh Father, Oh God, the Father!
"You could never do such things.
"First you'd need a mother
one no one honors,
one who toils in the dirt
one who gives and gives of her love."
One day I cursed that mother-fucking God.

Translated by Jayant Karve and Eleanor Zelliot with Pam Espeland

Waman Nimbalkar

Waman Nimbalkar-1

MOTHER

Just as the day sank down and the dark's kingdom came
We would sit at the door with no light in the hut.
In house after house the lamp would be lit,
The fire would be started, bhakri kneaded,
From somewhere the smell of lentils, of vegetables,
would hit our noses. In our stomachs all was darkness.
And a stream of tears would flow from my eyes.
The darkness was split, a dull shadow came toward us.
As she walked, the burden on her head shook, shifted.
Dark, dark slender body- this was my mother.
Drudged in the woods for sticks from morning on.

All we brothers, sitting, waiting, watching, for her.
And if she didn't sell the wood, all of us slept hungry.
One day something happened, how, we never understood.

Mother came, foot wrapped, blood flowing down.
A huge black snake had bitten her, two women said.
It showed its hood, struck, then slowly crawled away.
Mother was laid on the mat, the charmed cord tied,
the mantras said, the village vaidya called.
Day went, and as it went, life went from her body.

Waman Nimbalkar-2

Our wailing broke out, became thin in the air.
Mother had gone, leaving her children in the wind.

My eyes seek my mother. I still grieve
I see a thin vendor of wood. I buy her sticks.

Translated by Vidyut Bhagwat and Eleanor Zelliot

Waman Nimbalkar-3

CASTE

When I knew nothing, I knew
My caste was low.
The Patil had kicked my father,
Cursed my mother.
They did not even raise their heads.
But I felt this 'caste' in my heart.
When I climbed the steps to school
Then too I knew my caste was low.
I used to sit outside, the others inside.
My skin would suddenly shiver with little thorns,
My eyes could not hold back the tears.

Our lips must smile when they cursed.
I don't understand anything--
I heard this, I learned that,
I became a man like a man.
Even now I don't know--
How is caste? Where is it?
It isn't seen so does it live inside the body?
All the questions float like smoke,
And the wick of thought is sputtering.
But when I knew nothing, then I knew
My caste was low.

Translated by Graham Smith

Waman Nimbalkar-4

WORDS

Words it is that set aflame houses, homes, countries.
Men as well.
Words extinguish even the fire
in men set aflame by words.
Were it not for words, the sparks of fire
would not have fallen from men's eyes,
great floods of tears would not have flowed
No one would have come near
nor have gone far away-
were it not for words

Translated by Graham Smith

Daya Pawar

Daya Pawar-1

BUDDHA

I never see you
in Jetawana's garden
sitting with closed eyes
in meditation, in the lotus position;
or
in the caves of Ajanta and Elora
with stony lips sewn shut
taking the last sleep of your life
I see you
walking, talking,
breathing softly, healingly,
on the sorrow of the poor, the weak;
going from hut to hut
in the life-destroying darkness
torch in hand,,
giving the sorrow
that drains the blood
like a contagious disease
a new meaning

Translated by Vidyut Bhagwat, Jayant Karve, and Eleanor Zelliot

Daya Pawar-2

THE GODS OF OCHRE

All that was yours was devastated
so the Gods of the Godhouse

who pitted fate on your forehead
were flung into the little stream.
Ten heads turned in ten directions
like the festival play at the time of Bohad.
Why did the thirty-three crores of Gods
dancing arrogantly in the back alley
come to life again?

Lighting the torch in broad daylight,
brandishing weapons in eight hands,
panting with bloody tongues,
they beat the drums of tradition.

You say you want to flee
this ghost-ridden town!
Oh yes, but how can you run far enough?
You may go anywhere, but wherever you ste
you will stumble over the ochre-colored Gods.

Translated by Jayant Karve and Eleanor Zelliot

Daya Pawar-3

THE CITY

One day someone dug up a twentieth-century city.
It's lying there now like a wade of paper
crumpled by a gigantic fist.
In it are traces of the "machine age"-
wheels, pieces of metal,
smokestacks like old cigarette butts.

If it weren't for these,
the place would be another Mohenjodaro.
Pick a spot, any spot, and dig a foot down.
You'll find stones, rocks, images covered with ochre,
some with elephant trunks sticking out of their faces,
some with tails hanging from their behinds.
Good! The museums will be filled this year.
Why don't we stuff these holy puppets for future generations?
Here's an interesting inscription:
"This water tap is open to all castes and religions."
What could it have meant?
That this society was divided?

Daya Pawar-4

That some were high while others were low?
Well, all right, then this city deserved burying-
Why did they call it the machine age?
Seems like the stone age in the twentieth-century.

Translated by Jayant Karve and Eleanor Zelliot with Pam Espeland

Daya Pawar-5

FOUR POEMS:1 - HIROSHIMA

Deep, deep in a cave
a straggling thread of light,
a hand of tenderness,
a lamenting cry for liberation breaks out,
but I am unguided;
a wave of superficial laughter-
even this is wiped away.
In lush green moss
my feet are deceived.
Stifled in my throat, my breath
struggles in my rib-cage;
let fall some devastating lightning-flash!
Let a bier be built for this existence!
And let it be annihilated
like Hiroshima.

Daya Pawar-6

FOUR POEMS: 2-OH! GREAT POET

Oh Valmiki,
should you sing the praises of Ramarajya
because you're the great poet of poets?
Seeing the heron's wounded wing
your compassionate heart broke out in lament.
You were born outside the village
in a shunned neighbourhood...where misery itself was born,
never festooned with fruit or flower...
The dejected faces...furrowed with care...
Is it true never heard
their lament as they cried for liberation?
One Shambuk of your own blood
caught fire, rose in anger.
Oh great poet,
singing the praises of Ramarajya,
even there the icy cliff of inhumanity towered up
Oh great poet,
how then should we call you a great poet?
Had you written just one single verse
exposing this injustice, this outrage-
then would your name have been carved on our hearts.

Daya Pawar-7

FOUR POEMS: 3 - YOU WROTE FROM LOS ANGELES

"In the stores here, in hotels, about the streets,
Indians and curs are measured with the same yard-stick;
'Niggėrs,' 'Blacks!' --this the abuse they fling me,
and deep in my heart a thousand scorpions sting me."
Reading all this, I felt *so damn good*!
Now *you've* had a taste of what we've suffered
in this country from generation to generation.

Daya Pawar-8

FOUR POEMS: 4 - TREE

This tree I saw mangled with sorrow,
had roots as deep down as the Bodhi-tree's
But the Bodhi-tree flowered,
and this tree through all seasons was barren.
Torments threaten to snap its sinews;
leaves decay, like the fingers of leprosy;
what stump is this? To serve as a crutch
each branch grasps another.
Since Death does not come, it must endure Death's throes
This tree I saw mangled with sorrow

"Four Poems" were translated by Graham Smith

Daya Pawar-9

SANSKRIT

In hut after hut, total darkness.
Then the siren went off.
From the fourteen story Damodar
comes - what's this? -- a gleam of light.
What do you say :
They got a permit for light.
Sh! Sh!
Don't peep into their windows.
They've taken shelter under their beds.
Generation after generation

has arranged the plastic playtime
of that Great Divine Culture.
Now then they
stuff balls of cotton in their ears.
In hut after hut, whimpering,
the weeping of a broken heart,
disturbs their peaceful life!

Translated by Jyant Karve and Eleanor Zelliot

Daya Pawar-10

SIDDHARTHA NAGAR

O Siddhartha!
The shantytown named after you
in this twentieth century
has been struck by the tyrannical plough of power.
Each hut
is uprooted like a worthless stone.
A police van was driven
right over the signboard which carried your name.
Clothing in rags, the mats used as beds--
these huge earnings of upteen generations-
scattered by police clubs.
A bunch of naked little children,
screaming and moaning, came onto the road.
--Hey, call that woman in Delhi!
--Oh, somebody phone the minister!
--Oh, isn't it nice, dear. That hell in front of our apartment
is going away-

These were the voices we heard in the air.
Before our very eyes, the surrounding land was cleared.
In air conditioned glass apartments,

power has taken the pose of the three monkeys.
If anyone asks, the sahib has left with his Personal
Assistant.

O Siddhartha, did you know
a project is going on to change the hearts
of the bandits in Chambal valley;
and here in the cultured world
white collar inhumanity has reached a peak.
Your Anand and Sariputra,
see, see - they shelter under someone's awning.
-Let's go, take out five rupees each,
let's take a march to the center of power.-
Listen to these gangsters, living under your name.

O Siddhartha,
You made a tyrant like Angulimal
tremble.
We are your humble followers.

How should we confront
this ferocious Angulimal?
O Siddhartha,

Daya Pawar-12

If we fight tooth and claw,
Try to understand us.
Try to understand us.

Translated by Vidya Dixit, Jayant Karve and Eleanor Zelliot

Translators' Notes : the wild area of the Chambal Valley in North India, long known for its bandits, was the scene of much Gandhian activity during the period in which Pawar wrote this powm. "Gangsters" refer to Dalit politicians who collect money to protest slum clearance but do nothing. Anand and Sariputra were disciples of the Buddha, but here children's names. Angulimal was a fierce robber converted by the Buddha. See also Trymbak Sapkale's poem about Angulimal.

J.V. Pawar

J.V. Pawar-1

I HAVE BECOME THE TIDE

As the sand soaks up the water at the shore,
so my great sorrow.
How long will it be like the sand?
How long will it cry out from its obstinate will to exist?

As a matter of fact, it should have been in tide like the sea out there.
Much would have been gained by rolling over the drawfs around here.

Even the sea has a shore; why doesn't my sorrow have limits? Why didn't those who squeezed oil from the sand have any inkling of sorrow?

The wind that blows every day
that day yelled in my ear --
"women stripped"
"village boycott"
"men killed"
As it spoke, it gave me a mantra: "Make another Mahad!"
My hands now move toward the weapon on the wall.

J.V. Pawar-2

I'm now the sea; I soar, I surge,
I move out to build your tombs.
The winds, storms, sky, earth
Now are all mine.
In every inch of the rising struggle
I stand erect .

Translated by Jayant Karve and Eleanor Zelliot

Translator's Notes : the oil from the sand idiom is from the classical Brahman poet, Waman Pandit, and carries the implication that if you try hard enough you can squeeze oil from the sand. The mantra refers to the first satyagraha of the Ambedkar movement, that in Mahad in 1928 to drink water from a public reservoir. When that ended in violence, a later conference in Mahad was called, and the portions of the Hindu law book, Manusmriti, which justify untouchability, were burned.

J.V. Pawar-3

IT'S REDDENING ON THE HORIZON

These twisted fists won't loosen now
The coming revolution won't wait for you.
We've endured enough; no more endurance now.
Won't do letting down your blood's call to arms
It won't do:
    the seeds of revolution have been sown since long
    no use awaiting the explosion now;
    the fire-pit is ablaze; it's for tomorrow
    even if you take to your heels now
    no use; life's certainty is no more.
How will they snuff the fire within us?
How will they stop minds gone ablaze?
No more reasoning now;
    unreason helps a lot
    Once the horizon is red
What's wrong with keeping the door open?

Translated by P.S. Nerurkar

J.V. Pawar-4

NAKED MIND

Agreed, I don't have the kind of naked mind you do.
Mine never could dare to pour oil over a burning hut.
I, too, had lit a stove, here, in this very hut
to straighten out those bent hut-like.
These huts burn daily, chewing a morsel or two,
poised, as it were, to spit at the sun.

Cultured ladies walking lightly--you'll meet them everywhere,
dainty, offering themselves,
but mothers and sisters in huts
will pawn their mangalsutras
carelessly.

Go ahead. Beat the drums of chastity
or of shameless condemnation;
I feel nothing about it.

J.V. Pawar-5

I don't have the kind of naked mind you do;
I really don't

Translated by P.S. Nerurkar

Editors' Note: The mangalsutra is the wedding necklace of Maharashtrian women. Nerurkar's translation has been changed slightly.

Tryambak Sapkale

Tryambak Sapkale-1

ANGULIMAL

When I came into this world
I was crying,
the world was laughing.
Two hands carressed me,
on my back, on my stomach.

When I was crawling
I used to fall,
then get up,
supported by the little fingers
of those hands.

When understanding came,
I cried.
The world only laughed.
Two hands raised the whip
to my back, to my stomach.

As I ran through this
bounteous, plentiful land
my feet burned,
my mind wept.
I ran yelling for my life
Hoping to meet someone like Eknath.

Tryambak Sapkale-2

I met quite a few
who revered Eknath.

They were engrossed
In their *kirten*
My cry did not
enter their hearts.

Even the Sahara
has an oasis.
I ran in search of
something like an oasis.

I tried to catch hold of
this turning earth.
My hands were brushed off.
I fell.
The world laughed,
pointing its fingers at me.

Tears dried.
Feet froze.
Gathering all my strength,
I laughed at this world.
Ha...Ha...Ha...Ha...
There was a tremor in the earth
when I laughed.

Tryambak Sapkale-3

Hey--how come you
rabbit spawn aren't laughing anymore?
Those fingers that point at me
will become fingers dangling
from the garland around my neck.

Angulimal
I am Angulimal...
I am Angulimal---

Translated by Jayant Karve and Eleanor Zelliot

Translators' Notes : Eknath was a 16th century Marathi saint-poet who was especially compassionate to Untouchables. In the kirtan, a sermon by a devotee and group singing of the saint-poet's songs, form an important part of the Bhakti movement to which Eknath belonged. Angulimal, a robber and murderer in Buddhist legends, wore the little fingers of the people he had killed as a garland before his conversion by the Buddha. See also Saya Pawar's poem, Siddharthanagar, which uses the legend of Angulimal in a different way.

Tryambak Sapkale-4

EKLAVYA

The round earth.
A steel lever
in my hand.
But no leverage?
Oh Eklavya
you ideal disciple!
Give me
the finger you cut off;
that will be my fulcrum .

Translated by Jayant Karve and Eleanor Zelliot with the assistance of A.K. Ramanujan

Translators' Note : Eklavya, a low caste character in the Mahabharata, cut off his thum at the request of the Brahman archery teacher Drona, lest he best Arjuna at the game.

Tryambak Sapkale-5

DO YOU WANT TO BE A MOTHER

Atma, Parmatma, Parbrahma
Your shabby tent is raised on these three pegs.

All your life you've been only a woman;
You've never become a mother!

I can satisfy
Your hunger for motherhood.
Do you want to be a mother?
I am ready to be adopted.

Translated by Jayant Karve and Eleanor Zelliot with the assistance of A.K. Ramanujan

Translators' Notes : Atma, parmatma, parbrahma is a play on the Upanishadic theme of the individual soul, the over soul, and the ultimate brahman, the three joined to symbolize mother. The Marathi word we have translated "shabby tent" carries the connotation of the tent of a wandering prostitute.

Tryambak Sapkale-6

DAY

Don't despair, my girl.
Even these days will pass.
This day's day will pass.
This day's day will soon be done.
Our day is not far off.
Look, the day is with child!

Translated by Jayant Karve and Eleanor Zelliot with the assistance of A.K. Ramanujan

Navayan Surve

Narayan Surve-1

FOR I AM BRAHMA

I will protect all that belongs to Brahma,
all that is Brahma
I'll undo the knot of time.

I'll bring the world to my door
where it will frolic like a child.
I'll play lagori with the sun.

I'll tie up big clouds like cows outside my house.
I'll milk them to fill pots with ambrosia.

I'll hold the wind in my yard
where it will spin like a top.
I'll raise the rooftops of heaven.

I'll straighten out the bending sky,
single-handed
and punish whoever bent it in the first place!

The mole's mountain, the mountain's mole-
they're both inside of me.

Narayan Surve-2

For I am Brahma. I hold the world together-
I, the helpless one,
without even a room to call my own.

Translated by Jayant Karve and Eleanor Zelliot with the assistance of Pam Espeland

Translators' Note : Brahma here is the Marathi brahm (Sanskrit:brahman.) The Upanishadic concept that ultimate reality is the same reality as a human soul is at the base of Survey's irony.

Suggestions for Further Reading in English

Ambedkar, B.R. *Dr. Babasahab Ambedkar: Writings and Speeches*. Bombay: Government of Maharashtra Education Department, 1979--Many volumes.

Bhaware, N.G. "Dalit, Woman, and Writers." *Eve's Weekly* XXXIII:52 (Dec. 29--Jan 5, 1980):54-55.

Bhoite, Uttam and Anuradha. "The Dalit Sahitya Movement in Maharashtra: A sociological Analysis." *Sociological Bulletin* 26:1 (March 1977): 60-75.

Jayashree Gokhale-Turner. "Bhakti or Vidroha: Continuity and Change in Dalit Literature." *Journal of Asian and African Studies* 25:1-2 (1980): 29-40.

------ "The Dalit Panthers and the Radicalisation of the Untouchables." *Journal of Commonwealth and Comparative Politics* 17:1 (March 1979): 77-93.

Hovell, Laurie. "Namdeo Dhasal: Poet and Panther." *Bulletin of Concerned Asian Scholars* 23:2 (1991):77-83.

Hardikar, Vinay. "Profiles in Social Transformation: Five Dalit Autobiographies." *New Quest* 49 (January-February 1985):52-56.

Jogdand, Prahlad Gangaram. *Dalit Movement in Maharashtra*. New Delhi: Kanak Publications, 1991.

Joshi, Barbara, editor. *Untouchable: Voices from the* Dalit Liberation Movement London: Zed Books, 1986.

Karnik, D.B. "Dalit Panthers: *Radical Humanist* 44: 4 (july 1979): 23-26, 32.

Mahar, J.j Michael, editor. The Untouchables in Contemporary India. Tucson: University of Arizona Press, 1972. Includes stories by Anna Bhau Sathe and Shankkarrao Kharat and comment by Beatrice Miller.

Mehta, Harish, *"Dalit Panthers : Voices from the Street."* *Bombay* (January 7-21) 1981:40-43.

Murugkar, Lata. *Dalit Panther Movement in Maharashtra. Bombay* : Popular prakashan, 1991.

Punalekar, S.P. "Identities and Consciousness: An Overview of Dalit Literature in Maharashtra." *Man and Development* X:4 (December 1988):111-140

Ramteke, D.L. *Revival of Buddhism in Modern India,* New Delhi: Deep & Deep Publications, 1983.

South Asia Bulletin VII: 1 & 2 (1987). Includes articles by Gail Omvedt and Barbara Joshi as well as poetry, some of which is re-published in this volume.

Vagartha 12 (1976). Includes an article by Eleanor Zelliot poetry re-published in this volume and a long poem by Waman Nimbalkar, and a short story by Baburao Bagul.

Zelliot, Eleanor. *From Untouchable to Dalit: Essays on the Ambedkar Movement* New Delhi: Manohar, 1992.

------ and Philip Engblom, editors. "A Marathi Sampler." *Journal of South Asian Literature* 17:1 (1982). Translations of Shankarrao Kharat, Baburao Bagul as well as poetry included in this volume and a critical article on Namdeo Dhasal by Dilip Chitre. Bibliography of Marathi literature in English which includes all *dalit* literature then Published.